Discover the
Dinosaurs

PLANT
EATERS

Joseph Staunton and Luis Rey

W
FRANKLIN WATTS
LONDON · SYDNEY

First published in 2009 by Franklin Watts

Text copyright © Franklin Watts 2009
Illustrations copyright © Luis Rey 2009

Franklin Watts
338 Euston Road
London NW1 3BH

Franklin Watts Australia
Level 17/207 Kent Street
Sydney, NSW 2000

Editor: Jeremy Smith
Design: Nicola Liddiard
Art director: Jonathan Hair
Consultant: Dougal Dixon MSc

Every attempt has been made to clear copyright. Should there be any inadvertent omission please apply to the publisher for rectification.

A CIP catalogue record for this book
is available from the British Library.

Dewey number: 629.47

ISBN 978 0 7496 8715 1

Printed in China

Franklin Watts is a division of
Hachette Children's Books,
an Hachette UK company
www.hachette.co.uk

Contents

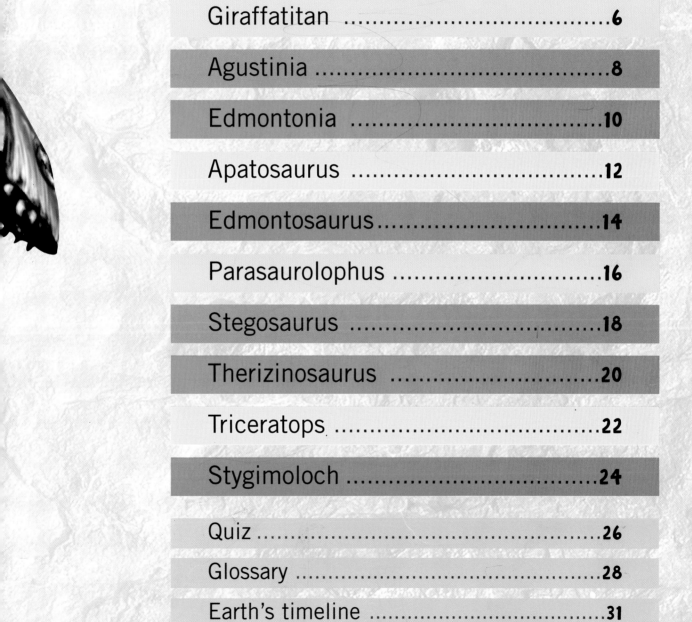

A world of dinosaurs

The world we live in is around 4.5 billion years old. Scientists know that there has been life on Earth for around 3.6 billion years because of **fossils** they have found. Some of these fossils were creatures called **dinosaurs**.

The age of the dinosaurs

Dinosaurs were the most famous group of animals to **evolve** in **prehistoric** times. They were the largest land-living creatures that have ever lived. Alongside them lived many smaller, bird-like dinosaurs, monsters of the oceans and massive flying **reptiles**. We know about these creatures because of the fossil remains they left behind. Dinosaurs lived in different **periods** of time, shown in the timelines below and at the back of this book.

A changing world

The Earth at the beginning of the age of the dinosaurs was very different from how it looks now. It was made up of one big **supercontinent** called **Pangea**.

Dinosaurs evolved and spread out across this supercontinent during the **Triassic** period. That is why fossils of the same type of dinosaurs can be found around the edges of the continents. Dinosaurs lived by the seaside, on river banks and in desert **oases** during Triassic times, and grazed on the branches of trees such as **conifers**. In the **Jurassic** period, the **climate** got milder and moister, and more dinosaurs started to appear. These included bigger plant eaters – **herbivores** – the topic of this book.

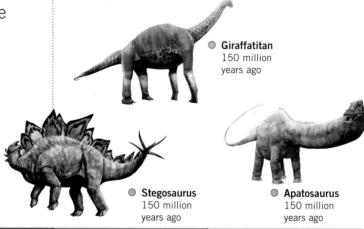

Giraffatitan
150 million years ago

Stegosaurus
150 million years ago

Apatosaurus
150 million years ago

227 millions of years ago	**205**		**180**		**159**	
		Lower		Middle		Upper
UPPER TRIASSIC			JURASSIC			

Triassic world Most of Earth's land is joined together in a single supercontinent.

Cretaceous world The supercontinent starts to split up.

Cretaceous changes

Over time, Pangea began to split up and dinosaurs started to change. By the end of the **Cretaceous** period, the dinosaurs that lived in North America looked very different from those in South America, and those in Europe, Asia and Africa. **Vegetation** changed, too. Flowering plants sprung up all over the world, and different types of dinosaurs able to eat these evolved.

Destruction!

Then, 65 million years ago, the dinosaurs were quite suddenly all wiped out.

Scientists think that this may have been caused by the impact of an enormous **meteor** that struck in Mexico. The only dinosaurs that survived were the bird-like (**avian**) dinosaurs, who were able to burrow, swim or dive to escape the catastrophic effects of the meteor impact. After the dinosaurs came a new age – the age of the **mammals** (and that includes people).

Parasaurolophus
75 million years ago

Triceratops
65 million years ago

Edmontosaurus
65 million years ago

Edmontonia
70 million years ago

Stygimoloch
65 million years ago

Therizinosaurus
70 million years ago

Agustinia
110 million years ago

144	98	65
Lower	Upper	

CRETACEOUS

Giraffatitan

Giraffatitan (arm lizard) was a giant **sauropod** that lived in Africa during the late Jurassic period. It was one of the largest animals ever to walk the Earth. It gets its name because of the fact that its 'arms' were longer than its legs.

🐾 PREDATORS

A healthy adult *Giraffatitan* probably had no **predators**, because of its size. The largest-known meat eater of that time was *Allosaurus* (pictured far right), which was less than half the size of this gentle giant.

Dino-Data

Height	8 metres
Length	25 metres
Weight	54,500 kg

◔ NECK

Giraffatitan used its long neck to reach up and chop off the tops of tall trees. It swallowed its food whole, without chewing it.

◔ SENSE OF SMELL

Giraffatitan had nostrils on the top of its head, and large nasal passages. This means that it probably had an excellent sense of smell, perfect for sniffing out the juiciest leaves.

Agustinia

Agustinia (Agustinia lizard) was a heavily armoured dinosaur that lived during the early Cretaceous period in South America. Its fossils were discovered in Argentina in 1997.

☣ ARMOUR

Agustinia had spikes and plates running right down the centre of its back. Some soared to heights of nearly 2 metres. Agustinia would probably have used its armour to scare off predators and attract **mates**.

🐾 RARE SPECIES

Only a few parts of this dinosaur have been found by fossil hunters. They include bones from the back, hips, legs and tail, and nine of Agustinia's amazing plates and spikes.

Dino-Data

Height	4.5 metres
Length	15 metres
Weight	4,072 kg

Edmontonia

Edmontonia (lizard from Edmonton) was a huge, tank-like dinosaur that lived during the late Cretaceous period. It was one of the last armoured dinosaurs on Earth. Fossilised skeletons have been found in Canada.

Dino-Data

Height	2 metres
Length	7 metres
Weight	4,000 kg

🐾 TERRITORY

Male *Edmontonia* fought with other males for **territory** and mates. Bigger males used their large shoulder spines for shoving contests.

🐾 DIET

Edmontonia had pouches in its cheeks, used for storing food. It also had a sharp beak that it used to slice through tough plant material.

🦶 ARMOUR

This creature wore the perfect defence for protection from **carnivores** – body armour! It was covered from head to toe with spikes and plates. Its only weakness was its soft belly.

Apatosaurus

Apatosaurus (deceptive lizard) was one of the longest animals ever to walk the Earth. It lived during the late Jurassic period in North America, and was a slow, lumbering giant.

🐾 TAIL

If any animal was brave enough to attack *Apatosaurus*, it would be making a big mistake. This dinosaur could defend itself by using its long tail as an enormous whip.

Dino-Data

Height	3 metres
Length	23 metres
Weight	22,680 kg

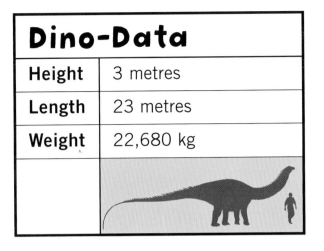

☝ NECK

Some people think *Apatosaurus* used its 12-metre-long neck to graze across large areas of vegetation. Others think that it poked up into the top of trees to reach fresh leaves.

Edmontosaurus

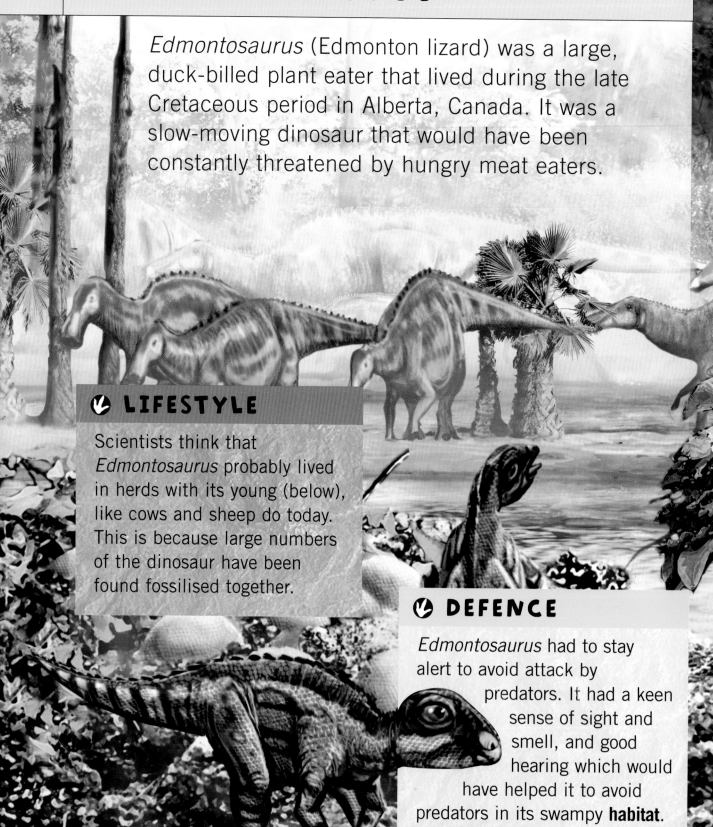

Edmontosaurus (Edmonton lizard) was a large, duck-billed plant eater that lived during the late Cretaceous period in Alberta, Canada. It was a slow-moving dinosaur that would have been constantly threatened by hungry meat eaters.

✔ LIFESTYLE

Scientists think that *Edmontosaurus* probably lived in herds with its young (below), like cows and sheep do today. This is because large numbers of the dinosaur have been found fossilised together.

✔ DEFENCE

Edmontosaurus had to stay alert to avoid attack by predators. It had a keen sense of sight and smell, and good hearing which would have helped it to avoid predators in its swampy **habitat**.

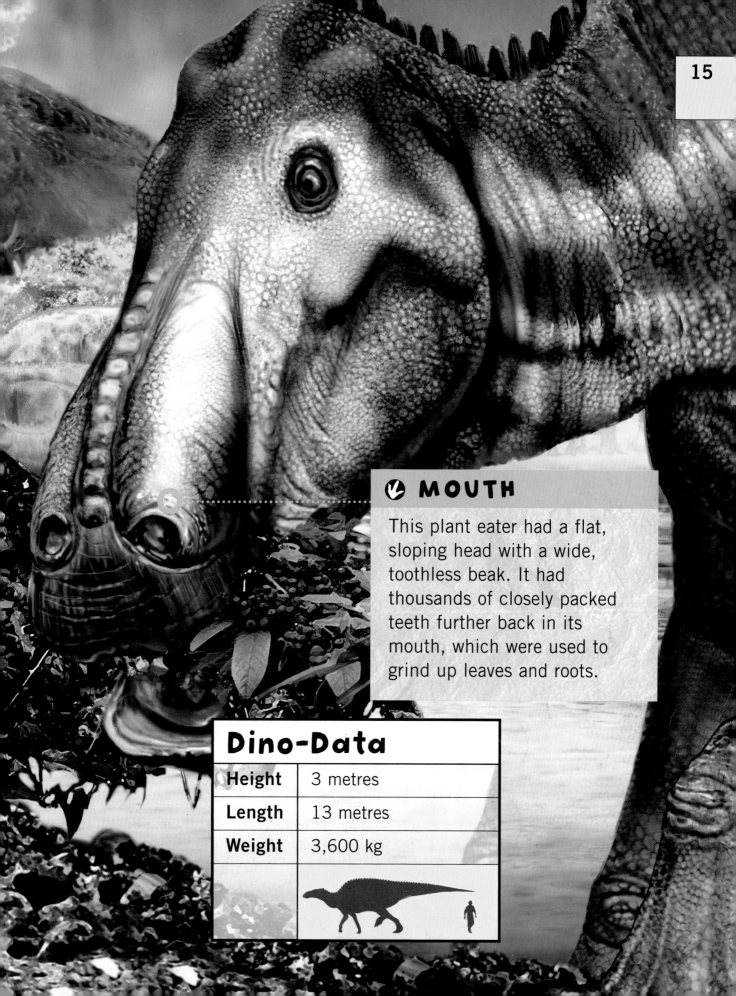

❤ MOUTH

This plant eater had a flat, sloping head with a wide, toothless beak. It had thousands of closely packed teeth further back in its mouth, which were used to grind up leaves and roots.

Dino-Data

Height	3 metres
Length	13 metres
Weight	3,600 kg

Parasaurolophus

Parasaurolophus (crested lizard) was a duck-billed dinosaur with a striking bony crest on the top of its head. It lived in North America during the late Cretaceous period.

☑ MOVEMENT

From the moment it was born, *Parasaurolophus* walked and ran on two legs, and could move quite quickly. It dropped to all fours to eat, and may have also spent some time in the water.

Dino-Data

Height	3 metres
Length	13 metres
Weight	3,600 kg

CREST

Parasaurolophus's hollow crest was nearly 2 metres long. It was probably used to attract a mate, and may even have been able to make a sound a bit like a foghorn.

DIET

Scientists have found fossilised *Parasaurolophus* stomachs. They show that this dinosaur ate a **diet** of pine needles, leaves and twigs.

Stegosaurus

Stegosaurus (covered lizard) was a plated dinosaur that lived in western North America during the late Jurassic period. It was a heavily built creature, about the size of a bus.

PLATES

Stegosaurus had between 14–22 bony plates running down its back. They may have been used to stop the dinosaur getting too hot or cold, or perhaps to attract a mate by changing colour.

TAIL

Stegosaurus had giant spikes at the end of its flexible tail. These would have made an excellent weapon to fight off predators such as this *Allosaurus* (right).

Dino-Data

Height	4 metres
Length	9 metres
Weight	2,000 kg

🐾 BRAIN

Stegosaurus had a very tiny brain – about the size of a walnut. This is very small in relation to the size of the dinosaur, and meant that this dinosaur was extremely low in intelligence.

Therizinosaurus

Therizinosaurus (scythe lizard) lived in the late Cretaceous period in Mongolia. When the first fossils were found in 1940, scientists thought they belonged to a giant turtle. When more remains were discovered, however, it was obvious that they belonged to a much stranger creature.

🐾 BODY PARTS

Therizinosaurus had a small head, a long neck, a short tail and a large body. It was such a strange shape that it could not have been a very fast runner.

Dino-Data

Height	5 metres
Length	9.6 metres
Weight	3,600 kg

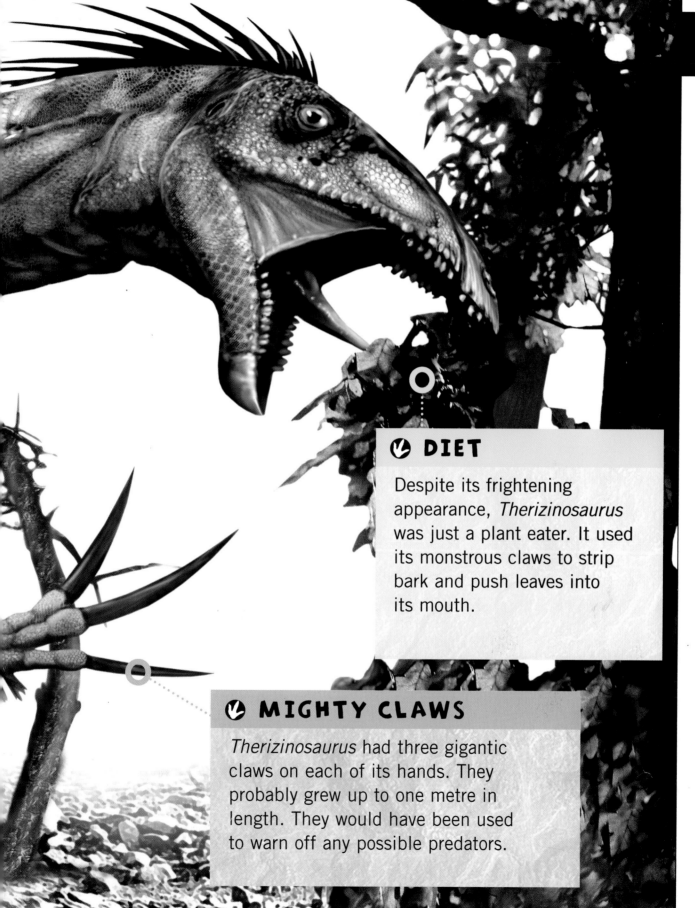

🐾 DIET

Despite its frightening appearance, *Therizinosaurus* was just a plant eater. It used its monstrous claws to strip bark and push leaves into its mouth.

🐾 MIGHTY CLAWS

Therizinosaurus had three gigantic claws on each of its hands. They probably grew up to one metre in length. They would have been used to warn off any possible predators.

Triceratops

Triceratops (three-horned face) was a rhinoceros-like creature that lived in North America during the late Cretaceous period. It was one of the last dinosaurs ever to live on Earth.

🐾 BIG HEAD

Triceratops had a 2-metre long skull, one of the largest of any land animal. Its enormous head was nearly a third of the size of its body.

Dino-Data

Height	2.9 metres
Length	7.9 metres
Weight	5,500 kg

⚡ DEFENCE

Triceratops had a giant head frill. This protected its neck from attack from dinosaurs such as this **Tyrannosaurus**. It was brightly coloured to make the animal look big and fierce from the front.

Stygimoloch

Stygimoloch (horned devil from the river of death) lived at the end of the Cretaceous period. It roamed alongside *Tyrannosaurus* and *Triceratops* in the Western United States. In 1995, a complete skeleton of this dinosaur was found.

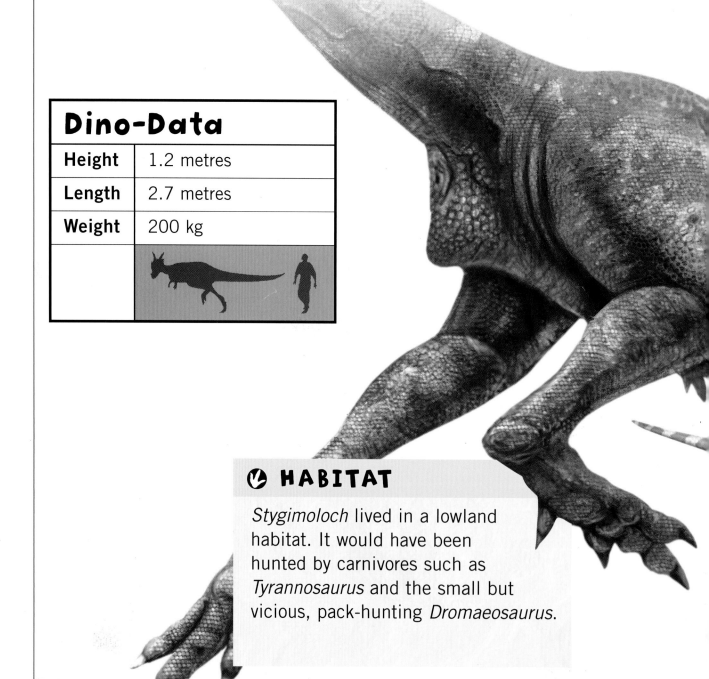

Dino-Data

Height	1.2 metres
Length	2.7 metres
Weight	200 kg

🐾 HABITAT

Stygimoloch lived in a lowland habitat. It would have been hunted by carnivores such as *Tyrannosaurus* and the small but vicious, pack-hunting *Dromaeosaurus*.

🐾 HEAD BUTT

In the past, people thought male *Stygimoloch* used their heads as battering rams to fight off predators. Today, scientists think they were used to joust with other *Stygimoloch* for female attention, like stags do today.

🐾 WALK

Stygimoloch walked upright and probably had small forelimbs and a long, stiff tail. It was capable of running at great speeds.

Quiz

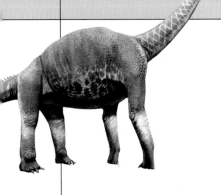

GIRAFFATITAN (ji-RAF-a-Tie-ton)

◑ What kind of dinosaurs hunted *Giraffatitan*?
◑ Why is it called an arm lizard?
◑ What period of time did *Giraffatitan* live in?
◑ Where did it live?

AGUSTINIA (ah-goo-STIH-nee-uh)

◑ When was *Agustinia* discovered?
◑ How tall were its spikes?
◑ What period of time did *Agustinia* live in?

EDMONTONIA (ed-mon-TON-ia)

◑ Where have *Edmontonia* fossils been found?
◑ How did this dinosaur cut up plant material?
◑ How did males fight?
◑ What was *Edmontonia's* one weakness?

APATOSAURUS (uh-PAT-oh-sore-us)

◑ How long was this dinosaur's neck?
◑ What period of time did it live in?
◑ What kind of food did it eat?
◑ How did *Apatosaurus* protect itself from attack.

EDMONTOSAURUS (ed-mon-to-SAW-rus)

◑ Where did *Edmontosaurus* live?
◑ Did it live in groups or alone?
◑ What type of habitat did *Edmontosaurus* prefer?
◑ What period of time did this dinosaur live in?

PARASAUROLOPHUS (par-ah-sawr-OL-o-fus)

- What was this dinosaur's most amazing feature?
- What did *Parasaurolophus* eat?
- What period of time did it live in?
- Did it move on two legs or four?

STEGOSAURUS (steh-gah-SAW-rahs)

- What period of time did this dinosaur live in?
- How big was its brain?
- How long did *Stegosaurus* grow?
- How many plates did it have along its back?

THERIZINOSAURUS (ther-ih-sen-oh-SAWR-us)

- What period of time did this dinosaur live in?
- What did scientists first think when they discovered fossils of this creature?
- How long were *Therizinosaurus*'s claws?

TRICERATOPS (trie-SER-a-tops)

- What period of time did this dinosaur live in?
- How big was its skull?
- What did *Triceratops* use its head frill for?
- What does the name *Triceratops* mean?

STYGIMOLOCH (STIG-ih-MOE-lock)

- What period of time did this dinosaur live in?
- What does the name *Stygimoloch* mean?
- Where did this dinosaur live?

Glossary

Avian: Relating or related to birds.

Cambrian: A period of time between 570–500 million years ago.

Carnivore: An animal that feeds on meat.

Climate: All the weather conditions at a place measured over a long period of time.

Conifer: A type of tree bearing cones and evergreen, needle-like or scale-like leaves.

Cretaceous: The period of time between 144–65 million years ago.

Diet: The food an animal eats.

Dinosaur: An extinct reptile that lived during the Mesozoic period.

Evolve: The development of different kinds of lifeforms from earlier varieties.

Fossil: Remains or impression of a prehistoric animal or plant embedded in rock.

Habitat: A place where a creature lives.

Herbivore: An animal which only eats plants.

Jurassic: The period of time between 180-144 million years ago.

Mammal: An animal that gives birth to live young and feeds its young with milk.

Mate: A female dinosaur chosen by a male to make babies with.

Mesozoic: A period of time between 230–65 million years ago.

Meteor: A rock from space.

Oases: Small, green areas in a desert region, usually with water.

Pangea: The name given to the supercontinent that existed at the

beginning of the age of the dinosaurs.

Period: A division of time distinguished by the sorts of animals and plants that lived then. A period usually lasts for tens of millions of years.

Predator An animal that eats other animals.

Prehistoric A name given to the period of time before the arrival of humans.

Quarternary: Period of time from 1.6 million years ago to the present day.

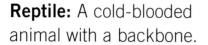

Reptile: A cold-blooded animal with a backbone.

Sauropods: A group of large, four-legged, herbivorous dinosaurs. They had very long necks, small heads with blunt teeth, a small brain, and long tails for balance.

Supercontinent: The single landmass that existed at the time of the dinosaurs (see Pangea).

Territory: An area of land fought over by males of a species. The winner has the right to mate with females that live there.

Triassic: Period of time between 227–180 million years ago.

Tyrannosaur: A large, carnivorous dinosaur that lived in the Late Cretaceous period.

Vegetation: Plants that can be eaten.

Earth's timeline

The history of the Earth dates back over 4 billion years. Scientists divide this time into periods. The earliest period of time is the **Cambrian** period. Dinosaurs appeared on Earth from the Triassic to the Cretaceous periods. Mammals, including humans, appeared in the **Quarternary** period.

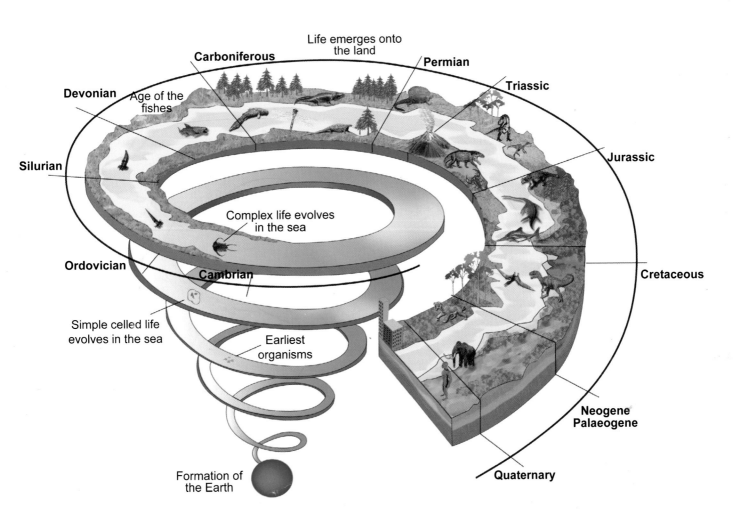

Index